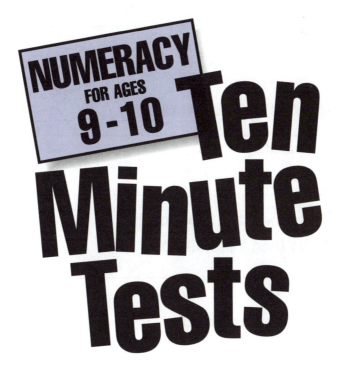

NUMERACY FOR AGES 9-10

Ten Minute Tests

CONTENTS

Test 1 Numbers (1)

Test 2 Multiplication and division (1)

Test 3 Measurement problems

Test 4 Fractions

Test 5 Ratio

Test 6 Data (1)

Test 7 Shape (1)

Test 8 Measures

Test 9 Addition and subtraction (1)

Test 10 Understanding numbers

Test 11 Place value

Test 12 Multiplication and division (2)

Test 13 Problems

Test 14 Decimals

Test 15 Shape (2)

Test 16 Data (2)

Test 17 Measures and area

Test 18 Addition and subtraction problems

Test 19 Money problems

Test 20 Divisibility

Test 21 Place value: decimals

Test 22 Multiplication

Test 23 Division

Test 24 Fractions and decimals

Test 25 Percentages

Test 26 Data (3)

Test 27 Shape (3)

Test 28 Time

Test 29 Addition and subtraction (2)

Test 30 Numbers (2)

Answers

Paul Broadbent and Peter Patilla

Test 1 — Numbers (1)

There are **10 digits**: 0, 1, 2, 3, 4, 5, 6, 7, 8, 9.
These are used to build up numbers.
Each digit in a number has a different value.

tens of millions	millions	hundreds of thousands	tens of thousands	thousands	hundreds	tens	units

If a number has **4 digits** then it is **thousands**.
If a number has **7 digits** then it is **millions**.

Colour in your score on the testometer!

Write these using numbers and words.

1. seventy-four thousand

2. two million five hundred thousand

3. sixty-three thousand eight hundred and five

4. 5,050,500 _____

5. 8,600,080 _____

Write the value of the digit which is in bold.

6. 5 8 **2** 9 4 _____

7. 6 **2** 9 1 0 _____

8. 7 **2** 0 4 8 2 _____

9. 1 **8** 4 0 3 7 3 _____

10. **9** 3 7 1 0 3 6 _____

Test 2 — Multiplication and division (1)

Multiplication **can** be done in any order.   8 x 6 = 6 x 8

Division **cannot** be done in any order.   35 ÷ 5 is **not the same** as 5 ÷ 35

Multiplication and division are opposites.
8 x 6 = 48
48 ÷ 6 = 8
48 ÷ 8 = 6

Colour in your score on the testometer!

Use the information above to check your answers.

1.   9 x 8 =
2.   8 x 7 =
3.   6 x 7 =
4.   5 x 8 =
5.   9 x 6 =
6.   54 ÷ 6 =
7.   72 ÷ 9 =
8.   56 ÷ 8 =
9.   63 ÷ 7 =
10. 32 ÷ 4 =

Test 3 — Measurement problems

You need to know **equivalent measurements** like these.

| 1km = 1000m | 1m = 1000mm | 1 tonne = 1000kg |
| 1m = 100cm | 1l = 1000ml | 1kg = 1000g |

When writing measurements, the decimal point separates the whole units from the parts of a unit.

3·5kg (3 **whole** kg)

2·25l (2 **whole** litres)

Fill in the missing amounts.

1. 4250 ml = ☐ litres
2. 1500 g = ☐ kg
3. 6750 mm = ☐ m
4. 2600 m = ☐ km
5. 1300 kg = ☐ tonne
6. 350 g + ☐ g = 1 kg
7. 540 mm + ☐ mm = 1 m
8. 125 ml + ☐ ml = 1 litre
9. 640 m + ☐ m = 1 km
10. 710 kg + ☐ kg = 1 tonne

Colour in your score on the testometer!

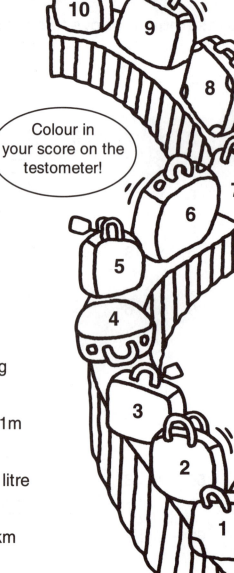

Test 4 — Fractions

Equivalent fractions look different but are both worth the same.

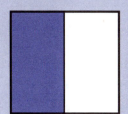

$\frac{1}{2}$ $\frac{2}{4}$ $\frac{4}{8}$

= means **equal** $\frac{1}{2} = \frac{2}{4}$
> means **greater than** $\frac{1}{2} > \frac{1}{4}$
< means **less than** $\frac{1}{4} < \frac{1}{2}$

Join to match the equivalent fractions.

1. $\frac{8}{12}$ — $\frac{1}{2}$
2. $\frac{4}{16}$ — $\frac{3}{4}$
3. $\frac{4}{8}$ — $\frac{2}{3}$
4. $\frac{2}{24}$ — $\frac{1}{4}$
5. $\frac{15}{20}$ — $\frac{1}{12}$

Make each statement true by writing <, > or =.

6. $\frac{3}{4}$ ☐ $\frac{9}{12}$
7. $\frac{1}{2}$ ☐ $\frac{6}{8}$
8. $\frac{2}{3}$ ☐ $\frac{4}{6}$
9. $\frac{1}{8}$ ☐ $\frac{1}{10}$
10. $\frac{9}{10}$ ☐ $\frac{3}{4}$

Colour in your score on the testometer!

Test 5   Ratio

Here, 2 out of 6 are coloured.

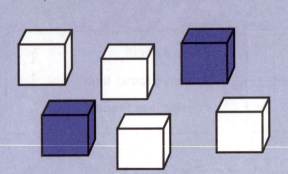

Of these sums, 6 out of 8 are correct.

2 x 3 = 6 ✓   9 x 2 = 20 ✗
6 x 4 = 24 ✓   6 x 3 = 18 ✓
4 x 5 = 20 ✓   7 x 8 = 50 ✗
7 x 7 = 49 ✓   10 x 4 = 40 ✓

Colour in your score on the testometer!

1. Colour 2 in every 3 squares.

2. Colour 3 in every 4 squares.
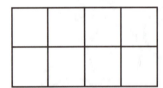

3. Colour 2 in every 3 squares.
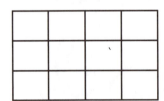

4. ☐ in every ☐ are coloured.
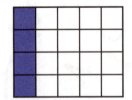

5. ☐ in every ☐ are coloured.
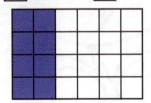

6. Draw 1 square for every 2 circles.
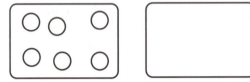

7. Draw 2 squares for every 1 circle.
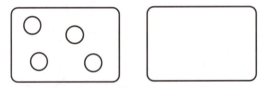

8. Draw 3 squares for every 2 circles.
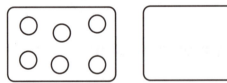

9. Draw 2 squares for every 3 circles.
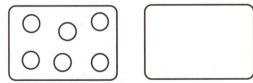

10. Draw 3 squares for every 4 circles.

Test 6 — Data (1)

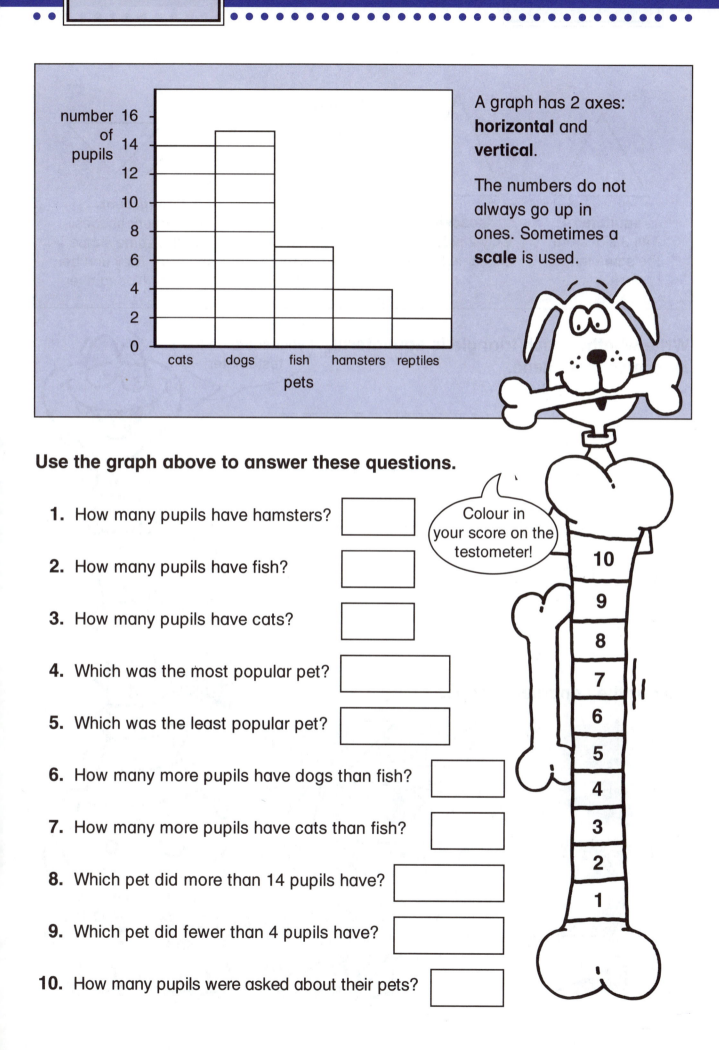

Use the graph above to answer these questions.

1. How many pupils have hamsters?
2. How many pupils have fish?
3. How many pupils have cats?
4. Which was the most popular pet?
5. Which was the least popular pet?
6. How many more pupils have dogs than fish?
7. How many more pupils have cats than fish?
8. Which pet did more than 14 pupils have?
9. Which pet did fewer than 4 pupils have?
10. How many pupils were asked about their pets?

Colour in your score on the testometer!

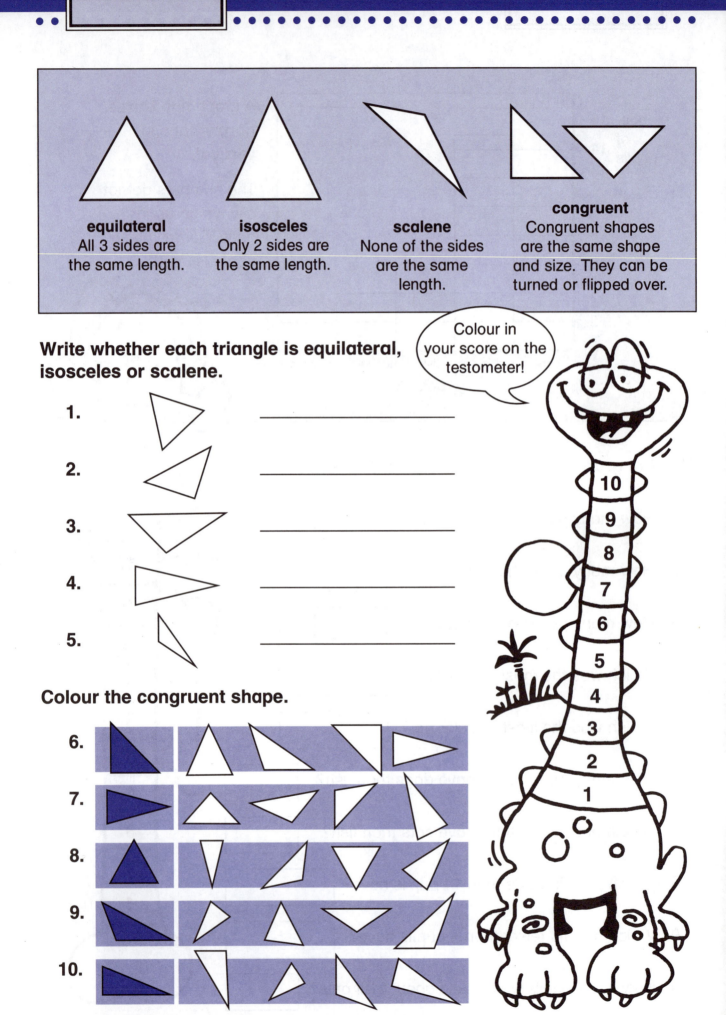

Test 8 | Measures

On **scales** you have to work out what each little division mark stands for.

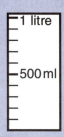

Each division mark stands for 100ml.   Each division mark stands for 250g.

Measure the volume.   **Measure the weight.**

1. 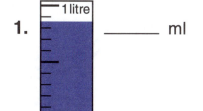 _____ ml   6. _____ kg
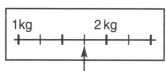

2. 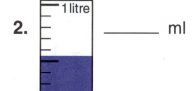 _____ ml   7. _____ kg
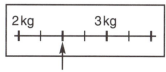

3.  _____ ml   8. _____ kg
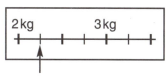

4. 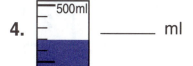 _____ ml   9. _____ g
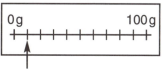

5. 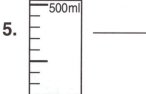 _____ ml   10. _____ g
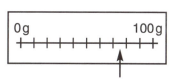

Colour in your score on the testometer!

Test 9 — Addition and subtraction (1)

Adding words: altogether, TOTAL, sum, add, more than, increase, plus

Subtracting words: less than, take away, minus, subtract, FEWER, decrease, difference

Colour in your score on the testometer!

Work out the anwers.

1. Add 353 to 34.

2. Total 35, 62 and 101.

3. What is the difference between 476 and 500?

4. Decrease 382 by 182.

5. What is 604 subtract 418?

6. What change would you get from £5 after spending £3.44?

7. Total 1·6m, 2·5m and 4·1m.

8. There were 225ml of liquid in a jug and 60ml was poured out. How much liquid was left?

9. Add £1.23, £2.75 and £1.35.

10. You have a 5·2m strip of ribbon. You need 1·75m to wrap your parcel. How much ribbon would be left?

Test 10 — Understanding numbers

Positive numbers are more than 0.

Negative numbers are less than 0.

These are **whole numbers**.

Fractional numbers come between whole numbers on a number line.

Write the missing numbers.

1. 3, 12, __, __, __, 48
2. 10, 1, __, __, __, −35
3. 6, 17, __, __, __, 61
4. −60, −45, −30, __, __
5. 5, −4, −13, __, __, __

Write whether these statements are true or false.

6. 7 − 4 gives a negative number.
7. 3 − 8 gives a negative number.
8. 7 ÷ 2 gives a fractional number.
9. 12 ÷ 3 gives a fractional number.
10. $1\frac{1}{2} + \frac{1}{2}$ gives a whole number.

Colour in your score on the testometer!

Test 11 — Place value

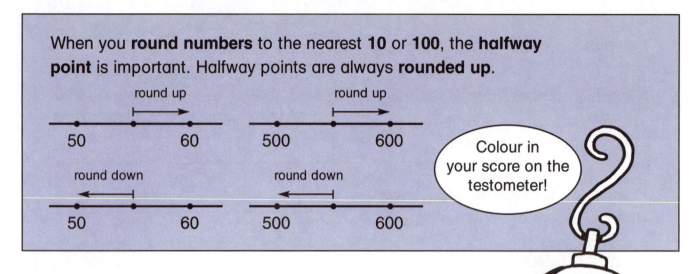

Round each number to the nearest 10.

1. 435 → nearest 10 →
2. 5718 → nearest 10 →
3. 1102 → nearest 10 →

Round each number to the nearest 100.

4. 2610 → nearest 100 →
5. 83954 → nearest 100 →

Make each number 10 more.

6. 799 → 10 more →
7. 1101 → 10 more →
8. 45612 → 10 more →

Make each number 10 times more.

9. 8020 → 10 times more →
10. 991 → 10 times more →

Test 12 — Multiplication and division (2)

The opposite, or inverse, of multiplication is division.

24 x 3 = 72 so 72 ÷ 3 = 24

The opposite, or inverse, of division is multiplication.

75 ÷ 5 = 15 so 15 x 5 = 75

Complete the number machine tables.

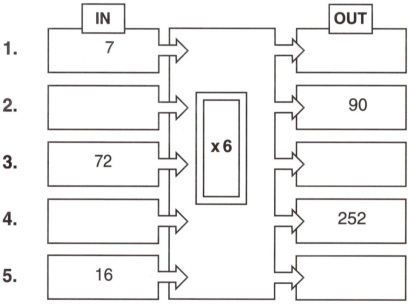

	IN		OUT
1.	7	x 6	
2.			90
3.	72		
4.			252
5.	16		

Write the missing numbers.

6.   40   x   ▭   =   240

7.   800 ÷   ▭   =   40

8.   30   x   ▭   =   1500

9.   60   ÷   ▭   =   2

10. 50   x   ▭   =   450

Colour in your score on the testometer!

Test 13 Problems

Tips for word problems
- Always read the problem carefully.
- Decide whether to add, subtract, multiply or divide.
- Writing a sum can help.
- Read the problem and ask, "Is my answer sensible?"

44p   15p   55p   20p   23p

Colour in your score on the testometer!

Answer these questions.

1. Nita buys 2 apples and 3 bags of crisps. How much change will she have from £1?

2. What is the difference in price between the most expensive item and the cheapest item?

3. If you buy one of each item, how much would you spend?

4. Which 2 items have a total cost of 67p?

5. How many bags of crisps can you buy for £1?

6. Lara has tins weighing 750g, 1500g and 450g in her bag. How heavy will her bag be?

7. There are 64 children in the choir. Half leave followed by a further 10. How many children are left in the choir?

8. A recipe for soup needs 1 onion, 220g mushrooms and 50ml of cream. Jack only wants to make half the amount. What measurements will he need?

9. Cherrie spends £50 on CD's. If each CD costs £5.99, how many can she buy?

10. Tim earns £3.50 a week. How many weeks will it take him to save £25?

Test 14 — Decimals

hundreds	tens	ones	(decimal point)	tenths	hundredths
2	4	3	•	2	5
200 +	40 +	3	+	$\frac{2}{10}$ +	$\frac{5}{100}$

Colour in your score on the testometer!

What is the bold digit worth in these numbers?

1. 3**5**·3 ⟹
2. 274·**2**1 ⟹
3. 0·**3**7 ⟹
4. **2**7·3 ⟹
5. 462·**9** ⟹

Write the number each arrow points to.

6.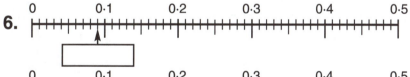

7.

8.

9.

10.

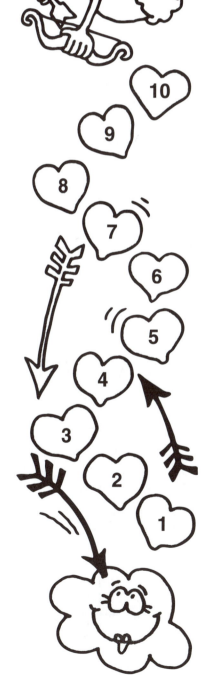

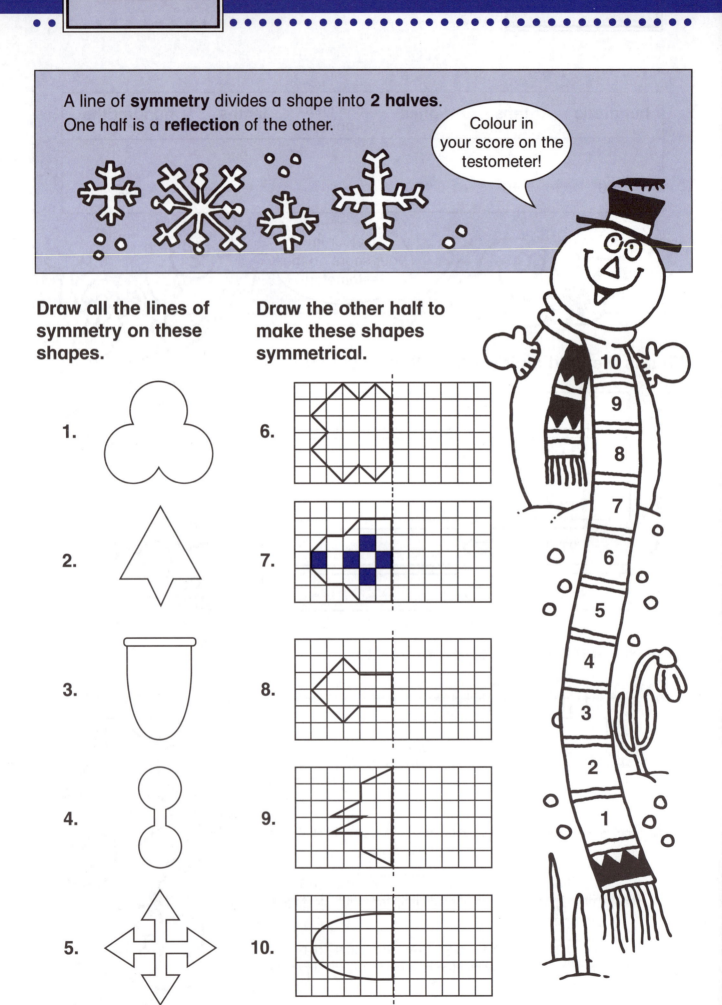

Test 16 Data (2)

When you collect information:

Mode is the number which occurs most often.

Range is the difference between the highest and lowest numbers.

Shoe sizes: 3½ 4 5 6 3½ 3½ 4 3 3½ 5

Mode is size **3½** (it occurs most often).

Range is **3** (difference between sizes 3 and 6).

Name		Ali	Ben	Clara	Den	Ella	Fran	Greg	Holly	Izzy	Juan
Age	years	10	9	11	10	9	11	11	10	9	9
	months	3		6		1		2	11	3	

Use the graph above to find the answers to these questions.

1. What is the mode? _____

2. What is the range? _____

3. Who is the eldest? _____

4. Who are the youngest? _____

5. Who is nearly 11? _____

6. Which children have had birthdays this month?
   _____

7. Whose birthday was last month? _____

8. Who has been 11 for 6 months? _____

9. How many children are older than Fran? _____

10. How many children are younger than Ali? _____

Colour in your score on the testometer!

Test 17 — Measures and area

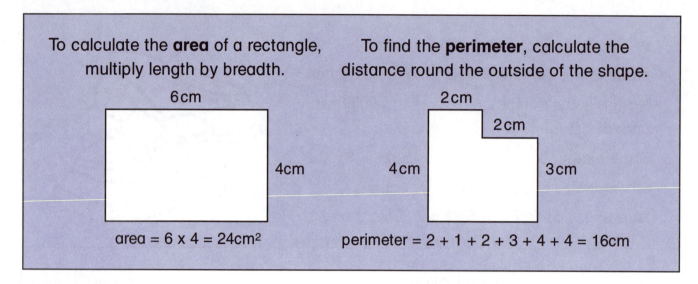

To calculate the **area** of a rectangle, multiply length by breadth.

area = 6 x 4 = 24cm²

To find the **perimeter**, calculate the distance round the outside of the shape.

perimeter = 2 + 1 + 2 + 3 + 4 + 4 = 16cm

Calculate the areas of these shapes.

Calculate the perimeters of these shapes.

Colour in your score on the testometer!

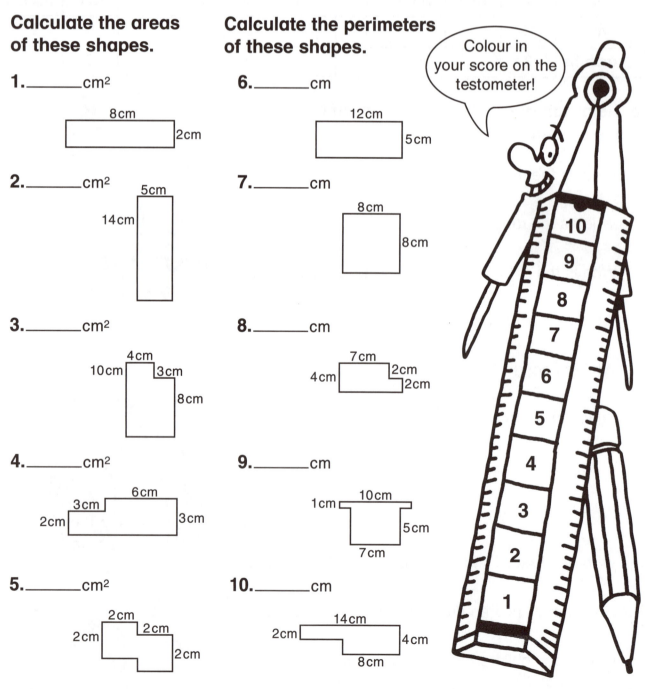

1. _____ cm²
2. _____ cm²
3. _____ cm²
4. _____ cm²
5. _____ cm²
6. _____ cm
7. _____ cm
8. _____ cm
9. _____ cm
10. _____ cm

Test 18 — Addition and subtraction problems

Odd numbers end in 1 3 5 7 9.
Even numbers end in 0 2 4 6 8.
Always check your answer.
Problems are usually a little more tricky to answer.

Colour in your score on the testometer!

| 64 | 230 | 71 | 36 | 770 | 159 |

Use the number line above to work out the answers.

1. Which pair total 100?
2. Which pair total 1000?
3. Which pair has a difference of 194?
4. What is the largest total with 3 numbers?
5. What is the smallest total with 3 numbers?

Answer these problems.

6. I thought of a number, then added 28. The total was 65. What was the number?
7. I thought of a number, doubled it and added 1. The answer was 33. What was the number?
8. I thought of a number, halved it and subtracted 1. The answer was 27. What was the number?
9. I thought of a number, subtracted 2 then doubled. The answer was 12. What was the number?
10. I thought of a number, added 4 then multiplied by 5. The answer was 70. What was the number?

Test 19 — Money problems

Do not mix **pounds** and **pence** when solving money problems. Work in either pounds or pence.

175p + 32p + 400p = £1.75 + £0.32 + £4.00 as pounds
             = 175p + 32p + 400p as pence

Colour in your score on the testometer!

Work out the answers.

1. How much change is there from £15 if you buy 3 items costing £2.99 each?

2. Total £3.84, £6.28 and £6.27.

3. How much change is there from £2 if you spend 62p, 15p and 33p.

4. Total 23p, £2.96 and 39p.

5. How much change is there from £20 if you buy 5 items costing 75p each?

Find the cost of 1 of each of these.

6. 5 cost £6.25
7. 7 cost £2.31
8. 9 cost £8.91

Find the cost of 6 of these.

9. 1 costs 95p
10. 1 costs £1.12

Test 20 Divisibility

For whole numbers:
- all even numbers are divisible by 2.
- if the last 2 digits are divisible by 4, the whole number is divisible by 4.
- if the last digit is 5 or 0, the whole number is divisible by 5.
- if the last digit is 0, the whole number is divisible by 10.
- if the digits total 9, the whole number is divisible by 9.

Write whether these are true or false.

1. 327 is divisible by 2 _____

2. 410 is divisible by 10 _____

3. 150 is divisible by 5 _____

4. 444 is divisible by 4 _____

5. 315 is divisible by 9 _____

Arrange the digits above to make 2 numbers that are divisible by:

6. 2 ⇒ ☐ ☐

7. 4 ⇒ ☐ ☐

8. 5 ⇒ ☐ ☐

9. 10 ⇒ ☐ ☐

10. 9 ⇒ ☐ ☐

Colour in your score on the testometer!

Test 21 — Place value: decimals

When you **multiply** a number by 10 the digits move 1 place to the **left**.

3·4   x 10 =   34·0
17·2 x 10 = 172·0
0·42 x 10 =   4·20

When you **divide** a number by 10 the digits move 1 place to the **right**.

3·4   ÷ 10 = 0·34
17·2 ÷ 10 = 1·72
0·42 ÷ 10 = 0·042

Write these numbers using decimals.

1. four point one six
2. fourteen point zero five
3. nought point two four
4. six and three hundredths
5. nine and nine tenths

Multiply these numbers by 10.

6. 5·6 x 10
7. 1·05 x 10
8. 0·06 x 10

Divide these numbers by 10.

9. 13·75 ÷ 10
10. 4·20 ÷ 10

Colour in your score on the testometer!

Test 22 — Multiplication

The boxes opposite show two ways to long multiply 25 x 37.

```
   2 5
 x 3 7
```

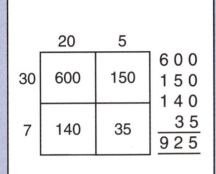

Answer these.

1. 36 x 24
2. 44 x 35
3. 28 x 19
4. 43 x 38
5. 66 x 47

Calculate the area.

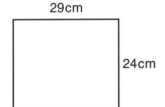

6. _____ cm²

7. _____ cm²

8. _____ cm²

9. _____ cm²

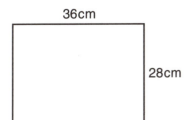

10. _____ cm²

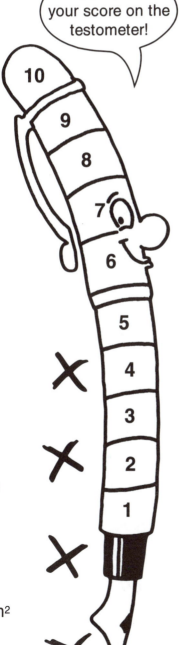

Colour in your score on the testometer!

Test 23 Division

The box opposite shows one way to divide 218 ÷ 9.

```
      2 4 r 2
9) 2 1 8
  -1 8 0    → (9 x 20)
     3 8
    -3 6    → (9 x 4)
        2   remainder
```

Work out these division problems.

1. 478 ÷ 5 =
2. 860 ÷ 7 =
3. 577 ÷ 4 =
4. 639 ÷ 9 =
5. 877 ÷ 6 =

Write the missing digit.

6.
```
    1 6 ▉
4) 6 7 6
```

7.
```
    7 7
5) 3 ▉ 5
```

8.
```
    ▉ 6
6) 3 9 6
```

9.
```
    2 7 5
3) ▉ 2 5
```

10.
```
     3 1
▉) 2 1 7
```

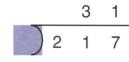

Colour in your score on the testometer!

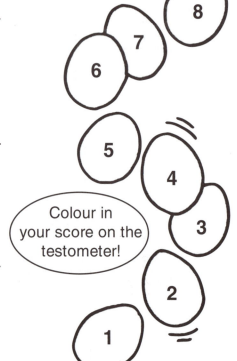

Test 24 — Fractions and decimals

$\frac{2}{3}$ of £150

Find $\frac{1}{3}$ first = £50

then $\frac{2}{3}$ = £100

$\frac{8}{12}$ can be cancelled. The numerator and denominator can be divided by 4.

$$\frac{8 \div 4}{12 \div 4} = \frac{2}{3}$$

Colour in your score on the testometer!

Write the answers.

1. $\frac{2}{3}$ of £171
2. $\frac{3}{4}$ of £136
3. $\frac{7}{10}$ of £450
4. $\frac{3}{8}$ of £632
5. $\frac{5}{8}$ of £712

Cancel each fraction. Make each one as simple as you can.

6. $\frac{4}{24}$
7. $\frac{24}{36}$
8. $\frac{30}{80}$
9. $\frac{25}{100}$
10. $\frac{40}{100}$

Test 25 — Percentages

% means **out of 100**.

$50\% = \frac{50}{100} = \frac{1}{2}$

$30\% = \frac{30}{100} = \frac{3}{10}$

10% of £7 = 70p

$\frac{10}{100}$ of £7 = 70p

$\frac{1}{10}$ of £7 = 70p

Write each % as a fraction.

1. 10% ➔
2. 25% ➔
3. 40% ➔
4. 60% ➔
5. 90% ➔

Calculate these percentages.

6. 20% of £230 ➔
7. 30% of £70 ➔
8. 25% of £80 ➔
9. 40% of £90 ➔
10. 75% of £120 ➔

Colour in your score on the testometer!

Test 26 — Data (3)

Graph to show the distance walked by Pam

On a line graph the points are joined up.

Colour in your score on the testometer!

Answer the following questions.

1. What time did Pam set off?
2. What time did she finish?
3. How far did she walk?
4. When did she stop for lunch?
5. How long was lunch?
6. When did Pam rest in the afternoon?
7. How long did she rest?
8. How long did it take her to walk 6km?
9. How long did it take her to walk 12km?
10. How long did it take her to walk 14km?

Test 27 — Shape (3)

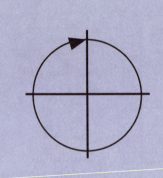
A complete turn is 4 right angles. It is 360°.

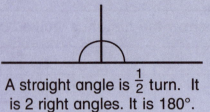
A straight angle is ½ turn. It is 2 right angles. It is 180°.

A right angle is ¼ turn. It is 90°.

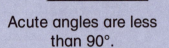
Acute angles are less than 90°.

Obtuse angles are between 90° and 180°.

Tick all angles that are less than 90°.

1. ☐
2. ☐
3.  ☐
4.  ☐
5.  ☐

What is the size of the missing angle?

6.  ☐
7. 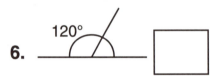 ☐
8.  ☐
9. ☐
10. ☐

Colour in your score on the testometer!

Test 28 — Time

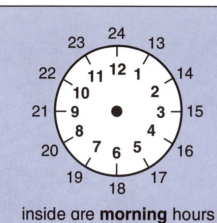

inside are **morning** hours
outside are **afternoon** hours

am times	pm times
morning hours	afternoon hours
midnight → noon → midnight	

Join the matching times.

1. 10.25   11.10 pm
2. 18.30   6.15 am
3. 23.10   10.25 am
4. 06.15   12.45 am
5. 00.45   6.30 pm

Write each time in the 24-hour clock time.

6. 4.30 pm → ___ . ___
7. 6.25 am → ___ . ___
8. 5.15 pm → ___ . ___
9. 10.20 am → ___ . ___
10. 11.55 pm → ___ . ___

Colour in your score on the testometer!

Test 29 — Addition and subtraction (2)

Some questions are easier to work out in your head than writing them down as sums.

It is quicker to answer 386 – 99 mentally than as a sum.

See which of these you can answer in your head.

1. Total 437 and 59.
2. Take 66 away from 385.
3. 3765 add 200.
4. 5793 subtract 50.
5. Increase 472 by 84.

Write the missing numbers.

6. 3·7 + ▓ = 5
7. 3 − ▓ = 1·5
8. 125 + ▓ = 500
9. 1000 − ▓ = 225
10. ▓ + 550 = 1000

Colour in your score on the testometer!

Test 30 — Numbers (2)

A squared number is one which is multiplied by itself.

5 x 5 is 5 squared ➜ 25 is a square number.

A short way of writing 5 squared is 5^2.

Answer these questions.

1. What is 6 squared?
2. What is 3 squared?
3. What is 9 squared?
4. 10^2 =
5. 11^2 =
6. ▢ x ▢ = 49
7. ▢ x ▢ = 144
8. ▢ x ▢ = 25
9. ▢ x ▢ = 225
10. ▢ x ▢ = 16

Answers

Test 1
1. 74,000
2. 2,500,000
3. 63,805
4. five million fifty thousand and five hundred
5. eight million six hundred thousand and eighty
6. two hundred (200)
7. sixty thousand (60,000)
8. twenty thousand (20,000)
9. eight hundred thousand (800,000)
10. nine million (9,000,000)

Test 2
1. 72
2. 56
3. 42
4. 40
5. 54
6. 9
7. 8
8. 7
9. 9
10. 8

Test 3
1. 4·25 litres
2. 1·5 kg
3. 6·75m
4. 2·6 km
5. 1·3 tonnes
6. 650g
7. 460mm
8. 875ml
9. 360m
10. 290kg

Test 4
1. $\frac{8}{12} = \frac{2}{3}$
2. $\frac{4}{16} = \frac{1}{4}$
3. $\frac{4}{8} = \frac{1}{2}$
4. $\frac{2}{24} = \frac{1}{12}$
5. $\frac{15}{20} = \frac{3}{4}$
6. =
7. <
8. =
9. >
10. >

Test 5
1.
2.
3.
4. 1 in every 5
5. 2 in every 6/1in every 3
6.
7.
8.
9.
10.

Test 6
1. 4
2. 7
3. 14
4. dog
5. reptile
6. 8
7. 7
8. dog
9. reptile
10. 42

Test 7
1. equilateral
2. isosceles
3. scalene
4. isosceles
5. scalene
6.
7.
8.
9.
10.

Test 8
1. 850ml
2. 550ml
3. 300ml
4. 350ml
5. 100ml
6. 1·75kg
7. 2·5kg
8. 2·25kg
9. 10g
10. 75g

Test 9
1. 387
2. 198
3. 24
4. 200
5. 186
6. £1.56
7. 8·2m
8. 165ml
9. £5.33
10. 3.45m

Test 10
The missing numbers are in **bold**.
1. 3 12 **21 30 39** 48
2. 10 1 **-8 -17 -26** -35
3. 6 17 **28 39 50** 61
4. -60 -45 -30 **-15 0 15**
5. 5 -4 -13 **-22 -31 -40**
6. false
7. true
8. true
9. false
10. true

Test 11
1. 440
2. 5720
3. 1100
4. 2600
5. 84000
6. 809
7. 1111
8. 45622
9. 80200
10. 9910

Test 12
1. 42
2. 15
3. 432
4. 42
5. 96
6. 6
7. 20
8. 50
9. 30
10. 9

Test 13
1. 1p
2. 40p
3. £1.57
4. crisps and fizzy drink
5. 4
6. 2700g
7. 22
8. $\frac{1}{2}$ onion
   110g mushrooms
   25ml cream
9. 8
10. 8

Test 14
1. five
2. one hundredth
3. three tenths
4. twenty
5. nine tenths
6. 0·09
7. 0·45
8. 0·33
9. 0·22
10. 0·05

Test 15
1.
2.
3.
4.
5.